ACCOUNTING LEDGER BOOK

Name: ______________________________

Phone: ______________________________

Year: ________

No.	Date	Description	Account	Payment (Debit)	Deposit (Credit)	Total

Year: ________

No.	Date	Description	Account	Payment (Debit)	Deposit (Credit)	Total

Year: ________

No.	Date	Description	Account	Payment (Debit)	Deposit (Credit)	Total

Year: ________

No.	Date	Description	Account	Payment (Debit)	Deposit (Credit)	Total

Year: ________

No.	Date	Description	Account	Payment (Debit)	Deposit (Credit)	Total

Year: ________

No.	Date	Description	Account	Payment (Debit)	Deposit (Credit)	Total

Year: ________

No.	Date	Description	Account	Payment (Debit)	Deposit (Credit)	Total

Year: ________

No.	Date	Description	Account	Payment (Debit)	Deposit (Credit)	Total

Year: ________

No.	Date	Description	Account	Payment (Debit)	Deposit (Credit)	Total

Year: ________

No.	Date	Description	Account	Payment (Debit)	Deposit (Credit)	Total

Year: ________

No.	Date	Description	Account	Payment (Debit)	Deposit (Credit)	Total

Year: ________

No.	Date	Description	Account	Payment (Debit)	Deposit (Credit)	Total

Year: ________

No.	Date	Description	Account	Payment (Debit)	Deposit (Credit)	Total

Year: ________

No.	Date	Description	Account	Payment (Debit)	Deposit (Credit)	Total

Year: ________

No.	Date	Description	Account	Payment (Debit)	Deposit (Credit)	Total

Year: ________

No.	Date	Description	Account	Payment (Debit)	Deposit (Credit)	Total

Year: ________

No.	Date	Description	Account	Payment (Debit)	Deposit (Credit)	Total

Year: ________

No.	Date	Description	Account	Payment (Debit)	Deposit (Credit)	Total

Year: ________

No.	Date	Description	Account	Payment (Debit)	Deposit (Credit)	Total

Year: ________

No.	Date	Description	Account	Payment (Debit)	Deposit (Credit)	Tota

Year: ________

No.	Date	Description	Account	Payment (Debit)	Deposit (Credit)	Total

Year: ________

No.	Date	Description	Account	Payment (Debit)	Deposit (Credit)	Total

Year: ________

No.	Date	Description	Account	Payment (Debit)	Deposit (Credit)	Total

Year: ________

No.	Date	Description	Account	Payment (Debit)	Deposit (Credit)	Total

Year: ________

No.	Date	Description	Account	Payment (Debit)	Deposit (Credit)	Total

Year: ________

No.	Date	Description	Account	Payment (Debit)	Deposit (Credit)	Total

Year: ________

No.	Date	Description	Account	Payment (Debit)	Deposit (Credit)	Total

Year: ________

No.	Date	Description	Account	Payment (Debit)	Deposit (Credit)	Total

Year: ________

No.	Date	Description	Account	Payment (Debit)	Deposit (Credit)	Total

Year: ________

No.	Date	Description	Account	Payment (Debit)	Deposit (Credit)	Total

Year: ________

No.	Date	Description	Account	Payment (Debit)	Deposit (Credit)	Total

Year: ________

No.	Date	Description	Account	Payment (Debit)	Deposit (Credit)	Total

Year: ________

No.	Date	Description	Account	Payment (Debit)	Deposit (Credit)	Total

Year: ________

No.	Date	Description	Account	Payment (Debit)	Deposit (Credit)	Total

Year: ________

No.	Date	Description	Account	Payment (Debit)	Deposit (Credit)	Total

Year: ________

No.	Date	Description	Account	Payment (Debit)	Deposit (Credit)	Total

Year: ________

No.	Date	Description	Account	Payment (Debit)	Deposit (Credit)	Total

Year: ________

No.	Date	Description	Account	Payment (Debit)	Deposit (Credit)	Total

Year: ________

No.	Date	Description	Account	Payment (Debit)	Deposit (Credit)	Total

Year: ________

No.	Date	Description	Account	Payment (Debit)	Deposit (Credit)	Total

Year: ________

No.	Date	Description	Account	Payment (Debit)	Deposit (Credit)	Total

Year: ________

No.	Date	Description	Account	Payment (Debit)	Deposit (Credit)	Total

Year: ________

No.	Date	Description	Account	Payment (Debit)	Deposit (Credit)	Total

Year: ________

No.	Date	Description	Account	Payment (Debit)	Deposit (Credit)	Total

Year: ________

No.	Date	Description	Account	Payment (Debit)	Deposit (Credit)	Total

Year: ________

No.	Date	Description	Account	Payment (Debit)	Deposit (Credit)	Total

Year: ________

No.	Date	Description	Account	Payment (Debit)	Deposit (Credit)	Total

Year: ________

No.	Date	Description	Account	Payment (Debit)	Deposit (Credit)	Total

Year: ________

No.	Date	Description	Account	Payment (Debit)	Deposit (Credit)	Total

Year: ________

No.	Date	Description	Account	Payment (Debit)	Deposit (Credit)	Total

Year: ________

No.	Date	Description	Account	Payment (Debit)	Deposit (Credit)	Total

Year: ________

No.	Date	Description	Account	Payment (Debit)	Deposit (Credit)	Total

Year: ________

No.	Date	Description	Account	Payment (Debit)	Deposit (Credit)	Total

Year: ________

No.	Date	Description	Account	Payment (Debit)	Deposit (Credit)	Total

Year: ________

No.	Date	Description	Account	Payment (Debit)	Deposit (Credit)	Total

Year: ________

No.	Date	Description	Account	Payment (Debit)	Deposit (Credit)	Tota

Year: ________

No.	Date	Description	Account	Payment (Debit)	Deposit (Credit)	Total

Year: ________

No.	Date	Description	Account	Payment (Debit)	Deposit (Credit)	Total

Year: ________

No.	Date	Description	Account	Payment (Debit)	Deposit (Credit)	Total

Year: ________

No.	Date	Description	Account	Payment (Debit)	Deposit (Credit)	Total

Year: ________

No.	Date	Description	Account	Payment (Debit)	Deposit (Credit)	Total

Year: ________

No.	Date	Description	Account	Payment (Debit)	Deposit (Credit)	Tota

Year: ________

No.	Date	Description	Account	Payment (Debit)	Deposit (Credit)	Total

Year: ________

No.	Date	Description	Account	Payment (Debit)	Deposit (Credit)	Tota

Year: ________

No.	Date	Description	Account	Payment (Debit)	Deposit (Credit)	Total

Year: ________

No.	Date	Description	Account	Payment (Debit)	Deposit (Credit)	Tota

Year: ________

No.	Date	Description	Account	Payment (Debit)	Deposit (Credit)	Total

Year: ________

No.	Date	Description	Account	Payment (Debit)	Deposit (Credit)	Tota

Year: ________

No.	Date	Description	Account	Payment (Debit)	Deposit (Credit)	Total

Year: ________

No.	Date	Description	Account	Payment (Debit)	Deposit (Credit)	Total

Year: ________

No.	Date	Description	Account	Payment (Debit)	Deposit (Credit)	Total

Year: ________

No.	Date	Description	Account	Payment (Debit)	Deposit (Credit)	Tota

Year: ________

No.	Date	Description	Account	Payment (Debit)	Deposit (Credit)	Total

Year: ________

No.	Date	Description	Account	Payment (Debit)	Deposit (Credit)	Total

Year: ________

No.	Date	Description	Account	Payment (Debit)	Deposit (Credit)	Total

Year: ________

No.	Date	Description	Account	Payment (Debit)	Deposit (Credit)	Total

Year: ________

No.	Date	Description	Account	Payment (Debit)	Deposit (Credit)	Total

Year: ________

No.	Date	Description	Account	Payment (Debit)	Deposit (Credit)	Tota

Year: ________

No.	Date	Description	Account	Payment (Debit)	Deposit (Credit)	Total

Year: ________

No.	Date	Description	Account	Payment (Debit)	Deposit (Credit)	Tota

Year: ________

No.	Date	Description	Account	Payment (Debit)	Deposit (Credit)	Total

Year: ________

No.	Date	Description	Account	Payment (Debit)	Deposit (Credit)	Tota

Year: ________

No.	Date	Description	Account	Payment (Debit)	Deposit (Credit)	Total

Year: ________

No.	Date	Description	Account	Payment (Debit)	Deposit (Credit)	Tota

Year: ________

No.	Date	Description	Account	Payment (Debit)	Deposit (Credit)	Total

Year: ________

No.	Date	Description	Account	Payment (Debit)	Deposit (Credit)	Tota

Year: ________

No.	Date	Description	Account	Payment (Debit)	Deposit (Credit)	Total

Year: ________

No.	Date	Description	Account	Payment (Debit)	Deposit (Credit)	Tota

Year: ________

No.	Date	Description	Account	Payment (Debit)	Deposit (Credit)	Total

Year: ________

No.	Date	Description	Account	Payment (Debit)	Deposit (Credit)	Tota

Year: ________

No.	Date	Description	Account	Payment (Debit)	Deposit (Credit)	Total

Year: ________

No.	Date	Description	Account	Payment (Debit)	Deposit (Credit)	Tota

Year: ________

No.	Date	Description	Account	Payment (Debit)	Deposit (Credit)	Total

Year: ________

No.	Date	Description	Account	Payment (Debit)	Deposit (Credit)	Tota

Year: ________

No.	Date	Description	Account	Payment (Debit)	Deposit (Credit)	Total

Year: ________

No.	Date	Description	Account	Payment (Debit)	Deposit (Credit)	Tota

Year: ________

No.	Date	Description	Account	Payment (Debit)	Deposit (Credit)	Total

Year: ________

No.	Date	Description	Account	Payment (Debit)	Deposit (Credit)	Tota

Year: ________

No.	Date	Description	Account	Payment (Debit)	Deposit (Credit)	Total

Year: ________

No.	Date	Description	Account	Payment (Debit)	Deposit (Credit)	Tota

Year: ________

No.	Date	Description	Account	Payment (Debit)	Deposit (Credit)	Total

Year: ________

No.	Date	Description	Account	Payment (Debit)	Deposit (Credit)	Tota

Year: ________

No.	Date	Description	Account	Payment (Debit)	Deposit (Credit)	Total

Year: ________

No.	Date	Description	Account	Payment (Debit)	Deposit (Credit)	Tota

Year: ________

No.	Date	Description	Account	Payment (Debit)	Deposit (Credit)	Total

Year: ________

No.	Date	Description	Account	Payment (Debit)	Deposit (Credit)	Tota

Year: ________

No.	Date	Description	Account	Payment (Debit)	Deposit (Credit)	Total

Year: ________

No.	Date	Description	Account	Payment (Debit)	Deposit (Credit)	Total

Year: ________

No.	Date	Description	Account	Payment (Debit)	Deposit (Credit)	Total

Year: ________

No.	Date	Description	Account	Payment (Debit)	Deposit (Credit)	Tota

Made in the USA
Las Vegas, NV
29 June 2023

74009617R00063